Jack and Stan

Written by
Debbie Strayer

Illustrations by
Joy Majewski

New Sounds:

bl
pl
cr

_ck
_ll

(Note: The pictures indicate the sound, not the spelling.)

Common Sense Press

© 1998 by Common Sense Press

Printed 09/15

8786 Highway 21 • Melrose, FL 32666

ISBN 1-880892-59-6

The pets are at the vet.
They met in the pen.

1

Jack and Mack are black. Stan and Dan are tan.

Jack hit a tack in a crack. Stan fell on a stack of cans.

Jan is the vet. He can plan for the pack. He likes to help.

When can they get in the van? Jan will let them go back.

Ready, set, go! They can get back on track. They ran to the den.

You can bet they like the plan. Jan is a helping man.

The pets are glad they met Jan. He is the best vet yet!

New Words:

__ck	bl	cr	pl	__ll

black   black   crack   plan   fell

Jack

Mack

tack

track

crack

stack

pack

back

Stan   cans   pets   met   pen   let   set

den   bet   best   yet

New Sight Words:

when   them   ready   go   helping

Review Words:

likes	van	in	on	vet
they	can	will	of	get
are	ran	is	Dan	the
he	glad	hit	tan	a
help	at	and	Jan	to
man	for	you	like	